Linda — Happy Birthday
to a very special friend!
With love,
Catherine
2011

Washington D.C.

A PHOTOGRAPHIC PORTRAIT

PHOTOGRAPHY BY

Jake McGuire

First published in the United States
of America by:

Twin Lights Publishers, Inc.
10 Hale Street
Rockport, Massachusetts 01966
Telephone: (978) 546-7398
http://www.twinlightspub.com

ISBN 1-885435-45-2

10 9 8 7 6

Editorial by
Rebecca Dominguez
http://www.FreelanceWriters.us

Book design by
SYP Design & Production, Inc.
http://www.sypdesign.com

Printed in China

INTRODUCTION

This photographic portrait is a celebration of Washington, D.C., the capital city of the world's greatest democracy. Jake McGuire has not only captured the famous "post card" views of this great city, he has captured its many moods and seasons.

When you stroll along the well manicured paths and verdant lawns connecting the city's stately marble and stone buildings, it is hard to imagine a time when Washington had to struggle for its life. Indeed, the city is a microcosm of the wars and hardships Americans endured along the way to greatness—Washington was spared no pain.

The city of Washington

After our young government met briefly in Philadelphia, New York, and Princeton, Congress chose the Potomac River as a natural midpoint that would satisfy both our southern and northern states. The fact that George Washington's home was across the river in Mount Vernon was a definite plus.

People began referring to our new capital as "the city of Washington" around 1791, and the name stuck. Plans were soon underway to design what was envisioned to be a world-class city in the same league as London and Paris.

After the British torched the just-completed Capitol building during the War of 1812, the city went into a slump for decades. A congressional vote to abandon the capital narrowly lost by nine votes.

The Union shall go on...

Fifty years later, during the Civil War, many Washingtonians wanted to stop the construction of the new U.S. Capitol building. President Lincoln responded "If people see the Capitol going on, it is a sign we intend the Union shall go on."

The wise visionaries who protected the struggling city would be proud and astounded today. The broad avenues and streets on the original blueprints that writer Charles Dickens once dismissed as "a city in need of citizens," now have an international cultural and racial flavor. The government buildings where Americans work and the monuments where Americans remember have created a dazzling array of architecture at its finest moments.

Come now and visit Washington, D.C., at the beginning of a new century, through these vivid and beautiful photographs. Tour the 16 galleries and museums of the Smithsonian Institution. Visit the White House, our elegant monuments and memorials, our parks and playgrounds, our government buildings, our universities and cathedrals.

Come in the spring when the city is in full blossom for the famous Cherry Blossom Festival. Take a walking tour of historic neighborhoods like Dupont Circle and Georgetown.

Enjoy our nation's capital, a city with no equal in the world.

OPPOSITE

Washington Monument
The Washington Monument pierces a lavender-pink sky, casting its reflection on still waters.

Francis Scott Key Bridge

"O say can you see by the dawn's early light..."

The Francis Scott Key Bridge is named after the poet-lawyer who wrote the famous words of our National Anthem in 1814 during a valiant defense of Fort McHenry by American forces in the War of 1812.

Iwo Jima Memorial

This famous statue celebrates the successful capture by the Marines of the strategically vital Pacific island of Iwo Jima during World War II.

U.S. Capitol Rotunda

Under the majestic central dome of the Capitol is the Rotunda, a circular ceremonial space that also serves as an art gallery of historically significant works.

**Washington Monument with Smithsonian
Castle Fireworks**

Fireworks light up the dramatic turrets of the
Smithsonian Castle, while the top of the Washington
Monument blends in perfect harmony.

**U.S. Capitol and the Washington and
Lincoln Memorials**

At twilight, the famous shapes of Washington's
monuments to past presidents and the Capitol
are dramatized with lighting.

Smithsonian Castle

This imposing 12th century Norman-style tower shows off the rich, red sandstone building material, making the Castle one of the most interesting structures in Washington.

National Air and Space Museum

This museum maintains the largest collection of historic air and spacecraft in the world. One of the museum's two buildings is located on the National Mall.

Shakespeare Theatre Company

Located at the Lansburgh Theatre in the heart of Penn Quarter, this theatre company is one of the finest classic theatres since its founding in 1985.

U.S. Supreme Court

Rows of 16 classical Corinthian columns seem to "stand guard" at the Court's formidable entrance. The large scale of this neoclassical building conveys the importance and dignity of the nation's highest court as a coequal, independent branch of the United States Government.

Union Station
A Living and Working Museum

The grandeur of the new Beaux Arts railroad station helped place America's capitol city front and center on the international map. Visitors today are amazed at the craftsmanship of the station's 96-foot barrel-vaulted, coffered ceilings, adorned with 22-karat gold leaf.

Afternoon Light on Lincoln Memorial

This massive 19-foot statue of Lincoln by famous sculptor Daniel Chester French is center stage in the memorial chamber. French later added lighting to enhance the lines of the white Georgia marble figure.

LEFT

Lincoln Memorial

Carved in the wall behind Lincoln are the words, *"In this temple as in the hearts of the people for whom he saved the union the memory of Abraham Lincoln is enshrined forever."*

RIGHT

Jefferson Memorial

Thomas Jefferson was a vital part of every stage of the American Revolution, from defining the reasons for the colonies to break from Great Britain, to writing the Declaration of Independence, to serving as the first secretary of state and the third president.

Washington Monument in Autumn

The stark white monument pierces a clear blue sky in a bold setting of vibrant autumn leaves.

ABOVE

U.S. Capitol in Autumn

Autumn colors in our nation's capitol are especially dramatic in contrast to the city's many majestic, white buildings.

TOP

U.S. Capitol

Cherry blossoms grace the landscape with a profusion
of vibrant pink and white blossoms.

BOTTOM

Washington Monument

Colorful tulips create a beautiful springtime blanket
with the Washington Monument in the distance.

OPPOSITE

Washington Monument & Cherry Blossoms

The Cherry Blossom Festival is celebrated each spring,
when the blossoms are at their peak.

U.S. Capitol Architecture

The grand, neo-classical style of the Capitol is a visual feast of interesting architectural details, tall columns and balconies.

Old Executive Office Building
Pennsylvania Avenue

Its gingerbread windows and embellishments delight tourists today, but this grand Victorian-style building narrowly escaped the wrecking ball several times. It is now protected as a national historic landmark.

OPPOSITE

U.S. Supreme Court

The main entrance to the Supreme Court Building is
an elaborate oval plaza with marble inlaid walkways,
large statuary, fountains and colorful flower gardens.

ABOVE

Library of Congress

The dramatic details and embellishments of the 19th
century, Victorian-style Library of Congress delight
visitors to the largest library in the world. The magnificent domed Main Reading Room is worth the visit.

U.S. Capitol

Traffic swirls in ribbons of light and endless motion
while the Capitol sits solid, quiet, and reassuring.

4th of July Fireworks

What better place to view a celebration of our nation's
independence than the very place where our elected
officials ensure that our hard-fought liberty is secure.

Carousel on the Mall

The carousel on the National Mall is a favorite with children and is just one of many attractions and activities in this central Washington park.

Illuminated Jefferson Memorial

The swirling traffic ribbons show Americans on the move, a fitting setting for a monument to the president who spearheaded our nation's expansion westward from *"sea to shining sea."*

United States Navy Memorial and Heritage Center

Created by Stanley Bleifeld and located at 701 Pennsylvania Avenue, N.W, *The Lone Sailor*© stands watch on the plaza of the Navy Memorial. The memorial pays homage to all those who served, are currently serving, or who are yet to server in the Navy and other sea services.

TOP

Hay Adams Hotel

Across from the White House, this classic hotel takes its name from earlier residents of its site: John Hay, former Secretary of State for President Lincoln, and acclaimed author Henry Adams, descendant of two U.S. Presidents.

BOTTOM

Cherry Blossoms and Full Moon

The full moon casts a ghostly light on a profusion of cherry trees in full bloom around the Tidal Basin. These cultivated trees, a favorite in Japan, were a gift from the Japanese government in 1912.

Blue Night at Jefferson Memorial

The Jefferson Memorial pays tribute to Jefferson's many accomplishments as a revolutionary, a visionary, a president, author of the Declaration of Independence, and the promoter of Manifest Destiny. The memorial, modeled after the Pantheon, a 2nd century temple of worship in Rome, also reflects Jefferson's well-known personal tastes in architecture. It was Jefferson, himself, who introduced the classic styles of ancient Rome to a young capitol city. Inside, a 19-foot bronze statue depicts the president holding The Declaration of Independence.

American Flags

Chances are you'll find more American flags flying in
Washington than any other city in the nation.

Christmas at the White House

Every December, the President continues a
Washington tradition of lighting the National
Christmas Tree, just one of many beautiful decorations
at the White House.

The President's Helicopter

Marine One is caught mid-air by a fast shutter speed against the monolithic Washington Monument and U.S. Capitol. *"Marine One"* is the call sign used when the President is on board a helicopter from the U.S. Marine Helicopter Squadron 1. The Squadron provides transportation overseas and here at home for the President, the vice president, and occasionally Cabinet members and foreign dignitaries.

31

OPPOSITE

Lincoln Memorial

The Lincoln Memorial was built to resemble a Greek temple. It has 36 Doric columns, one for each state in America at the time of Lincoln's death.

ABOVE

Christmas at the Capitol

Ablaze with colorful lights, a majestic Christmas tree decorates the snow-covered lawn of the Capitol building.

American Flag

"I pledge allegiance to the flag of the United States of America and to the Republic for which it stands. One Nation under God, indivisible, with liberty and justice for all."

School children learn to pledge allegiance to it. Soldiers carry it into battle. It is flown at half-mast on somber occasions. It has been burned in protests both here and abroad. Flag Day honors it each year. It flies in front of government buildings, and it is given to grieving families at military funerals. "Old Glory", our nation's flag, is a powerful symbol of the greatest democracy in the world. To see it, high in the air as a breeze ripples through it, can bring tears of gratitude to American's eyes.

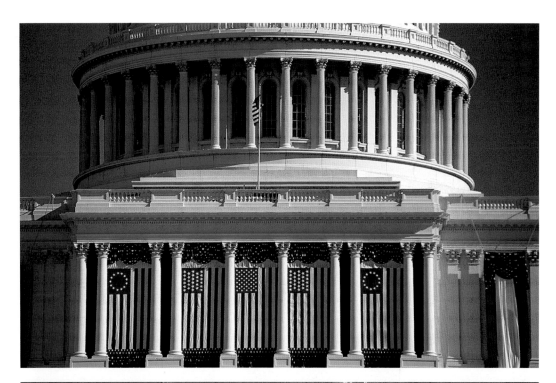

TOP

From Thirteen to Fifty Stars

As America grew, our flag changed from the original
circular pattern of 13 stars to straight rows of 50 stars.
Although the Continental Congress left no formal
record of the significance of the colors, it is said that
red symbolizes courage, white symbolizes innocence
and blue symbolizes justice.

BOTTOM

Teenagers at F.D.R. Memorial

The FDR memorial is a stirring reminder of the Great
Depression and the sacrifices of World War II.

U.S. Supreme Court

"Equal Justice Under the Law"

The seated figure in the foreground, The Contemplation of Justice, is framed by the intricate sculptures above the pediment's famous words.

U.S. Capitol Dome, Evening

Lit from within, against an evening sky, the Rotunda is 96 feet in diameter and rises 180 feet to the canopy, a shape that makes it one of the most easily recognizable buildings in the world.

White House in Summer

The term *"White House"* was first used by a congressman
in a letter to a colleague in 1812. The popular slang
remained a nickname until Theodore Roosevelt made
it official in 1901.

The National Archives

The National Archives building houses original copies
of the U.S. Constitution, the Bill of Rights, and the
Declaration of Independence.

Smithsonian Castle and Washington Monument

The tapered pillar of the Washington Monument
reaches for the sky in unison with the Romanesque-
Gothic towers of the Castle.

**Washington Monument and the Reflecting Pool
National Mall**

This 555-foot obelisk casts its watery shadow on the
reflecting pool. Weighing over 90,000 tons, this monument to George Washington is composed of white
marble and granite. In the 19th century, it was a long
climb up 897 steps to the observation area; today an
elevator whisks visitors to the top for a spectacular
view of the city.

Washington's Neoclassical Style

Architects in the new nation's capitol in the late 1700's and early 1800's understood that their mission was to design the greatest capital in the world since Ancient Rome. The new city's buildings, such as the U.S. Capitol, the White House, the Lincoln and Jefferson Memorials, all echo the Classical world with stately columns, pediments, friezes, and stark, white marble. The deliberate effect was to communicate a message of permanence, strength and solidity to the world and America.

U.S. Supreme Court at Dusk

Two marble statues at the entrance symbolize the powers of the highest court in the land. On the left, the female represents the Contemplation of Justice. On the right, the male figure is the Guardian or Authority of Law.

LEFT

Statuary Hall, U.S. Capitol

The National Statuary Hall in the Rotunda houses part of the Capitol's collection of statues donated by the states in commemoration of notable citizens.

RIGHT

Columns of Government Building

Reminiscent of architecture in the golden days of ancient Greek and Roman civilizations, Washington is a city of marvelous neoclassical architecture where entrances and porticos are graced with orderly rows of stately columns standing many stories tall.

TOP

Capitol Rotunda

The neoclassical style of the Rotunda, the central section of the Capitol building, is reminiscent of the Pantheon, a famous ancient Roman temple.

BOTTOM AND OPPOSITE

Jefferson Memorial

Thomas Jefferson struck a chord for human liberty 200 years ago that resounds through the decades. But in the end, Jefferson's own appraisal of his life, written on his tombstone, suffices: *"Author of the Declaration of American Independence, of the Statute of Virginia for religious freedom, and Father of the University of Virginia."*

U.S. Capitol Dome

An American flag flies in front of the building where
the Senate and House of Representatives work hard to
uphold the Constitutional rights of every American

The White House

Construction on the White House began in 1792 on
82 acres of land called The President's Park. John
Adams was the first presidential resident in 1800. Since
then, every president has further enhanced the interior
and the grounds.

U.S. Capitol at Christmas

The Christmas season lights up the halls of Congress
with trees, wreathes, and plenty of colorful lights.

TOP

F.D.R. Memorial

The statuary, shade trees, waterfalls, and quiet alcoves
of this expansive memorial on the National Mall create
the feeling of a secluded garden.

BOTTOM

Tribute to Ulysses S. Grant, National Mall

This large equestrian statue pays tribute to the famous
and victorius Civil War general who became America's
18th President.

OPPOSITE

Cherry Blossoms and Jefferson Memorial at Night

After the Jefferson Memorial was completed, 1,000
cherry trees were planted, transforming the grounds
into a strikingly beautiful area of our nation's capital.

Calder Mobile, National Art Gallery

The huge Alexander Calder mobile is an intriguing
invitation into the gallery's modern art exhibits.

BOTTOM

**Martin Luther King, Jr. Mural
D.C. Regional Library**

This powerful mural by artist Don Miller is a defini-
tive, visual documentation of Dr. King's great influence
on modern American society.

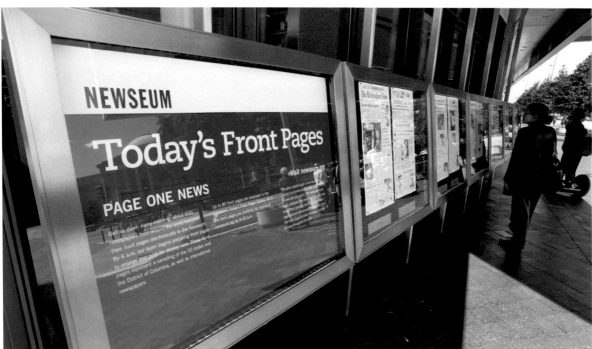

Newseum

The importance of the First Amendment is hard to miss at the museums 74 -foot-high marble engraved exterior. Located at 555 Pennsylvania Ave., N.W., the Newseum features galleries and theaters where visitors experience how the power of print is necessary to a democracy.

Smithsonian Castle Detail
"National Museum 1879"

Architect James Renwick Jr. may not have envisioned
that his provocative 19th century building would
become too small to house the museum's rapidly growing collections.

The Castle's fine details reflect the 12th century
Norman style that blended elements of late
Romanesque and early Gothic motifs.

Smithsonian Castle

The world-renowned Smithsonian Institution began in what is now known as Smithsonian Castle with a mysterious $500,000 donation in 1835 from the estate of James Smithson, a British scientist who had never set foot in the United States. Today the Smithsonian houses 16 museums and galleries, the National Zoo, and several research facilities.

53

TOP

Vietnam Women's Memorial

One of the most poignant memorial statues in
Washington honors nine military nurses and 58 civilian
women who were killed during the Vietnam War.

BOTTOM

Tomb of the Unknowns, Arlington National Cemetery

"Here rests in honored glory an American soldier known but to God"

Atop a hill overlooking Washington, the tomb originally held the remains of one unknown World War I
soldier. Since then, the remains of soldiers from later
wars have also been buried there.

OPPOSITE

Washington at Night

The photographer's lens merges the stark white facades
of three of Washington,s most famous structures—
Lincoln Memorial, Washington Monument and U.S.
Capitol— against a deep blue sky.

OLIVER ANDERSON
D AVERY • LONNIE A BROOKS
EN W CLARK • THOMAS D CLEM
RIAN G HUGHES • WILLIAM I INM
RVIN J KEISLING • MICHAEL L KIDD
ANSON • RICHARD M MARTIN
ALAN P PAGLIARONI • WILLIE L PON
SOLIZ • JAMES R SOUTHEY • ROG
ANDERSON • STERLING C BANKS
RTER • JIMMY RAY CLARK
NIELS • DARRELL W COT
UGLAS B FOURNET
PAUL V GRASSO
SON • JOHN E SWA
B LEAGUE • JERRY
MASK • R MAZURSKY
HN W MC HOMAS A McCOR
HARLES L PERR ROBERT G PRICE

Soldier Statue at Vietnam Memorial

This life-like bronze sculpture stands in a grove of trees near the west entrance to the Wall. The three soldiers represent the racial diversity of the troops.

Vietnam Veterans Memorial

The Vietnam Veterans Memorial is a hauntingly beautiful place that evokes powerful emotions. The smooth black granite walls are etched with the names of 58,200 men and women who died or are still missing. It is the most visited memorial in Washington.

Korean War Veterans Memorial

This powerful memorial, adjacent to the Lincoln
Memorial Reflecting Pool, honors the soldiers who lost
their lives *"...to defend a country they never knew and a people
they never met."* It features a life-sized, sculptured column
of 19 foot soldiers arrayed for combat, with the
American flag as their symbolic objective.

The Pentagon

The Pentagon is one of the world's largest office buildings, so large that the spacious U.S. Capitol Building
could fit into any one of the five wedge-shaped sections.

The United States Air Force Memorial

Three spires represent the core values of the Air Force
—integrity first, service before self, and excellence in
all that is done. Designed by James Ingo Freed and
located in Arlington, it is a tribute to the Air Force
and the organizations that came before it.

TOP

Iwo Jima Memorial

This sculpture is based on a Pulitzer-prize-winning photograph taken by an American photo-journalist during the intense World War II battle for the Pacific island of Iwo Jima.

BOTTOM

Arlington National Cemetery

Although the funerals of dignitaries at Arlington are often televised, the large majority of funerals at Arlington are private.

OPPOSITE

J.F.K. Gravesite and Arlington House
Arlington National Cemetery

President Kennedy once made an impromptu visit to Arlington House and remarked that the view of Washington was so magnificent that he could stay forever. Now the eternal torch burns on Kennedy's grave site on a gentle slope below the Arlington House. Our nation's youngest president is one of only two presidents buried at Arlington.

ABOVE

Arlington National Cemetery

Autumn leaves decorate the unending rows of graves in
our national cemetery. This peaceful setting is a final
resting place of honor for unknown soldiers, well-
known generals, astronauts, explorers, minorities, sci-
entists, doctors, writers, and supreme court justices.

OPPOSITE

Spring along the Potomac

Daffodils bloom along the Potomac River while a
gray blanket of fog settles along the Arlington
Memorial Bridge.

National Cathedral

The National Cathedral is the second largest cathedral in America and welcomes nearly 700,000 visitors and worshipers annually.

Union Station

Union Station's Beaux-Arts architecture brought a new grandeur to Washington in 1907 and set the stage for the next 40 years of Washington's classic architecture.

Albert Einstein

Einstein contemplates a map of the universe at the National Academy of Sciences. This informal statue pays fitting tribute to the most recognized scientist in the world, who is also honored as *"The Man of Century."*

OPPOSITE

Cosmos Club

This is not your typical social club. It was founded in 1878 as a center of good fellowship for the intellectually elite in the fields of art and science. Nobel and Pulitzer Prize winners are among its past and current members.

LEFT AND RIGHT

Four Season's Hotel

The Four Season's Hotel is located in historic Georgetown and is one of Washington's very best hotels. It is known for its luxury suits and over 1000 pieces of artwork that has been collected over 30 years by owner William Louis-Dreyfus.

Visitors at Tidal Basin

The tidal basin is irresistible for nature lovers when the
cherry trees are in full bloom. The profusion of these
famous pink and white blossoms transforms the landscape into a feast for all the senses.

Tidal Basin in Full Bloom

If cherry blossom time were a theatrical event, the
city's Tidal Basin would be "front-row center." Tens of
thousands of cherry trees in full bloom present their
colors along the water's edge leading up to the
Jefferson Memorial.

Mount Vernon

Understandably, George Washington once said, *"I can truly say I had rather be at home at Mount Vernon with a friend or two about me than to be attended at the seat of government by the officers of state and the representatives of every power in Europe."*

The Phillips Collection

The Phillips Collection is America's first museum of modern art. It is known for the exceptional quality of its collection and for the intimate environment in which art is experienced.

The International Spy Museum, 800 F Street

The recently renovated, but unassuming 19th-century façade of this building is a "covert" contrast to the updated interior. Each space creates a unique sense of the past as well as the modern and an atmosphere that enhances stories of espionage, exhibits of spy gadgets and hands-on activities. It's easy to believe that the Communist Party was once housed in this historic building located in the heart of the city.

INTERNATIONAL
SPY
MUSEUM

INTERNATIONAL
SPY
MUSEUM
STORE

INTERNATIONAL
SPY
MUSEUM
STORE

INTERNATIONAL SPY MUSEUM STORE

Watergate Office Complex

Seldom in the history of America has one word been so heavy with significance as the word, Watergate. It quickly stood for the shocking political scandal and constitutional crisis that began with the arrest on June 17, 1972 of five burglars who broke into Democratic National Committee headquarters at the Watergate Office Building. It ended two years later with the resignation of President Richard Nixon.

Georgetown University

Founded in 1789, the same year the U.S. Constitution took effect, Georgetown University is the nation's oldest Catholic and Jesuit university. Today Georgetown is a major international research university that prides itself in its commitment to justice and intellectual openness and character. The university was so deeply affected by the Civil War that when the war ended, the school adopted blue and gray as its official colors to symbolize the reunification of North and South.

Dupont Circle

Dupont Circle sits majestically at the intersection of several of Washington's busiest boulevards and is known for it's embassies, art galleries and night life.

OPPOSITE

Capitol in Summer

Summer blooms adorn the plaza on the Capitol grounds and complement the timeless beauty of this world-famous building.

LEFT

Jefferson Hotel

This historic hotel is four blocks from the White House and a mere stroll from other monuments, museums, and memorials. Although Thomas Jefferson never stayed here, his presence is definitely felt.

RIGHT

Dupont Circle

Dupont Circle is at the heart of this historic district which quickly became fashionable in the late 1800's. Today historic mansions line the broad avenues while row houses line the side streets.

Willard Hotel
The Residence of Presidents

Two blocks from the White House, this historic hotel
has hosted every U.S. President since Franklin Pierce
in 1850, as well as countless other dignitaries. After a
$120 million restoration, the hotel, previously closed
for 15 years, came back to life as the Willard Inter-
Continental Hotel in 1986. Crystal chandeliers, marble
columns, carved ceilings and reproductions of period
furnishings allow guests to fully appreciate the hotel's
storied past.

National Museum of Crime & Punishment

Visitors are introduced to the history of crime fighting, law enforcement, crime scene investigation, and punishment through interactive galleries within the museum.

**Basilica of the National Shrine of the
Immaculate Conception**

The largest Catholic Church in the Americas, the
National Shrine is home to more than 60 chapels and
oratories reflecting America's religious heritage and eth-
nic diversity. Adorned with a 329-ft tower, a brilliant
mosaic dome, stained glass windows, and polished stone
carvings, thousands of people visit every year.

Rainbow on the Potomac River Tidal Basin

After a summer rain, the tidal basin is graced with a rainbow arching high over this beautiful retreat in the heart of Washington.

St. John's Church

James Madison selected pew #54 in the early 1800's and unknowingly began a presidential tradition. Since then, pew #54 is reserved for the President. With its golden cupola and dome, St. John's Church enhances Lafayette Park with its history and classic style.

Memorial Bridge, Kennedy Center, and National Cathedral

Washington is so packed with history that one single photograph can capture several important monuments.

National Cathedral

The National Cathedral's magnificent, circular Rose
Window is 25 feet in diameter and represents the
power and glory of God and the mystery of creation as
depicted in over 10,000 pieces of stained glass.

Library of Congress

The Library of Congress has the largest book collection in the world, including a Gutenberg Bible and first
drafts of the Declaration of Independence and
Lincoln's Gettysburg Address.

Red, White, and Blue

A profusion of red and white azaleas frames the pure white dome of the U.S. Capitol against clear blue skies.

Georgetown Architecture

This fashionable street shows off a new nation's own distinct architectural style known as Federal-style. Erected in 1776-1820, residences like these were adapted from classical European architecture.

Georgetown Shops

Georgetown remains Washington's favorite, fashionable shopping area. It is the capital's center for famous citizens, as well as for restaurants, nightclubs, and trendy shops.

Alibi Club

The Alibi Club, built in the early 1800's, is one of Foggy Bottom's many landmark buildings and features Federal and Italianate architectural details. Privately owned today, it has always housed a business.

OPPOSITE

Ford's Theatre

History knows this theatre as the place where President Lincoln was assassinated. Today Ford's tireless Theatre Society has gone beyond that tragedy to reclaim it as a national treasure and a working theater. It's lively repertoire of plays and musicals celebrates America's multi-cultural heritage.

ABOVE

U.S. Holocaust Memorial Museum

This is America's national institution for the documentation, study, and interpretation of Holocaust history, and serves as our memorial to the millions of people murdered during the Holocaust.

The Georgetown Inn

Known for its old-style charm and elegance, the Georgetown Inn has been a favorite retreat for over 40 years for politicians, royalty and other celebrities.

Hillwood Museum and Gardens

Avid art collector and Post Cereal fortune heiress, Marjorie Merriweather Post gave her last estate and private art collection to the public for use as a museum. Her magnificent French and Russian collections are on view at Hillwood today.

Renwick Gallery
Smithsonian American Art Museum

Renwick Gallery is home to one of the nation's most extensive collections of American crafts and decorative arts from the nineteenth to the twenty-first centuries. In 1859, prominent banker William Wilson Corcoran needed a place to showcase his growing, private art collection. He hired James Renwick, Jr., architect of the Smithsonian Castle *(page 53).* Today the Gallery, with its distinctive mansard roofs, ornamental iron railings, pilasters, and pediments, is a National Architectural Landmark.

IRS Building

Award-winner for Historic Preservation and
Renovation, the IRS building is a fine example of 18th
Century French Renaissance architecture. It has been
updated to adapt and blend in with the different styles
of adjoining buildings of the Federal Triangle.

Folger Shakespeare Library

Henry Clay Folger and his wife, Emily, devoted their
lives to collecting Shakespeare's works and built a
museum for the public to enjoy. Today the library's
wider collections focus on 15th to 18th century British
and European history.

National Museum of the American Indian

This museum's architecture reflects the sensibilities of
Native communities across the hemisphere. A deep
connection to nature is evident in the structure from
its curvilinear, russet form evoking a wind-sculpted
rock formation, to its celestial east-facing entrance and
domed skylight. The integral landscape incorporates a
forest environment, wetlands, a meadow and a tradi-
tional crop garden complete with medicinal plants, as
well as placement of four large rocks at corners of the
grounds symbolizing the longevity, strength and scope
of the indigenous peoples within the hemisphere.

OPPOSITE

The White House

Marine One, the President's helicopter, approaches the South Lawn of the White House while the crowd below anticipates his arrival.

LEFT

The White House

The sophisticated, porticoed White House we see today is significantly larger and more elegant than the austere Georgian mansion designed over 200 years ago.

RIGHT

Federal Reserve Building

This handsome building (circa 1935) is headquarters to America's central bank which oversees our national monetary and financial system. The design is a modernistic approach to the more flamboyant Beaux-Arts style.

Old Executive Office Building

This Victorian-style building, originally built to house the State, War and Navy departments, is an outstanding example of the architectural and decorative taste of the late 1800's.

LEFT

Old Post Office Building

Another landmark building saved from the wrecking ball, the Old Post Office, built in 1899, offers guided tours and breathtaking vistas from atop its 315-foot clock tower.

RIGHT

The Textile Museum

One of the world's foremost specialized art museums, the Textile Museum is dedicated to promoting the understanding of creative achievements in the textile arts internationally.

ABOVE

U.S. Supreme Court Sculptures

Above the entrance to the Court is a symbolic group
of sculptures by artist Robert Aitken. The central figure is Liberty Enthroned, guarded on the left and right
by Order and Authority.

OPPOSITE

U.S. Supreme Court

Every year, inside this stately building, some 7,000
petitions must be reduced to less than 100 cases that
will be heard, a process one court historian calls
*"arguably the most important stage in the entire Supreme Court
process."*

Golden Silhouette

A vivid sunset transforms the familiar shapes of the
Washington skyline into pure gold, with its mirror
image in the Washington Monument's reflecting pool.

LEFT

The National Building Museum

The Great Hall is the centerpiece of this historic
building with ornate balconies and 75-foot Corinthian
columns. Formerly the U.S. Pension Building, many
presidential inaugural balls have been held here.

RIGHT

Old Town Alexandria

Leaves blanket the brick sidewalks and cobblestone
streets of Old Town, a popular tourist attraction with
restored 17th and 18th century residences and busi-
nesses just eight miles from Washington.

OPPOSITE

National Air & Space Museum
Smithsonian Institution

The Museum maintains the largest collection of historic air and spacecraft in the world which has grown to fill two separate, exhibition buildings.

LEFT AND RIGHT

National Air and Space Museum

The museum's exhibits trace man's love affair with flying from the Wright brothers, historic short flight above a North Carolina beach to the development of space craft that soar out of earth's gravitational field to take us to the moon and distant planets. Hundreds of artifacts include the original Wright 1903 Flyer, the Spirit of St. Louis, Blackbird, Enola Gay, Space Shuttles Enterprise and Apollo 11 command module. Museum visits can literally touch the moon, thanks to an actual lunar rock sample.

OPPOSITE

Final Salute

In the cold blur of a winter blizzard, a soldier gives a
final salute to a comrade during a military graveside
service at Arlington National Cemetery.

LEFT

Renwick Gallery in Winter

A recent snowfall highlights each structural detail of
this historic architectural landmark building, now
home to a prolific collection of American crafts and
decorative arts.

RIGHT

Benches on the Mall

Snow covers the benches along the tree-lined parkland
of The National Mall.

OPPOSITE

Georgetown and Key Bridge

Key Bridge crosses the Potomac to Virginia and
provides excellent views of the Washington and
Georgetown skylines. Pictured here are the spires
of Georgetown University.

ABOVE

The Old Stone House, Georgetown

This simple 18th century dwelling, one of the oldest
structures in Washington, is a popular museum of the
everyday life of middle-class colonial America. It's
beautiful English garden is a restive attraction for visitors in the busy shopping district of Georgetown.

Arlington Memorial Bridge

A rowing team hones their skills as they pass under the
Memorial Bridge. The bridge spans the Potomac River
connecting the Lincoln Monument in Washington
with Arlington National Cemetery in Virginia.

Potomac River and Georgetown

On a warm summer day, Washingtonians take to the
river with their own favorite water sport. The scenery
of Arlington on the west and Washington on the east
is filled with great views.

Dangerfield Island Marina

This popular marina in Alexandria, VA, also known as
the Sailing Marina, is a popular jumping off point for a
peaceful day of sailing the waters around Washington.

Francis Scott Key Bridge

The early morning light shines on Key Bridge and the tranquil Potomac River. To the left, the Key Bridge Marriott Hotel offers guests a lovely setting to reflect on the history of our democracy.

OPPOSITE

Navy and Marine Memorial

This statue of gulls in flight above a wave comes into view. In the Spring, a red carpet of tulips surrounds this dramatic memorial to Americans who served our country at sea.

LEFT AND RIGHT

The National Zoo

These sunbathing toothy reptiles and playful orang-utan are unaware that they live in one of the largest, state-of-the-art zoos in the world.

Kennedy Center

This world-class performing arts center, now in its 31st year, is America's living memorial to President Kennedy. It continues to fulfill Kennedy's vision by presenting a variety of performers from all over America and the world. Special programs also nurture new artists and provide art education.

Tribute to Ulysses S. Grant

This is the largest equestrian statue in the United States and the second largest in the world. Sculpted by H. M. Shrady and dedicated in 1922, it pays tribute to the victorious Civil War general who became America's 18th President. One of the greatest equestrians of his time, Grant was fearless in the heat of battle. This 252' x 69' monument depicts Grant, astride his horse, surrounded by a cavalry charge on the right and a battery of artillery on the left.

Rowers on Potomac River in Fog

An early morning rowing team paints a watery mark
in the heavy fog over the Potomac River with
Georgetown University hovering in the background.

Southwest Waterfront

This busy marina, near the confluence of the Potomac
and Anacostia Rivers, shows how much Washingtonians love their water sports. Across the river is
historic Fort McNair, which has been an active Army
post for over 200 years, third only to West Point and
Carlisle Barracks in longevity.

OPPOSITE

Illuminated Lincoln Memorial

The Lincoln Memorial stands alone in dignified silence
on the National Mall between the Capitol Building
and the Potomac River. The massive sculpture of
Lincoln faces a long, reflecting pool.

ABOVE

Washington Monument

The monument rises high above the camera lens in
this nighttime scene with the Capitol Building partially
hidden in the background.

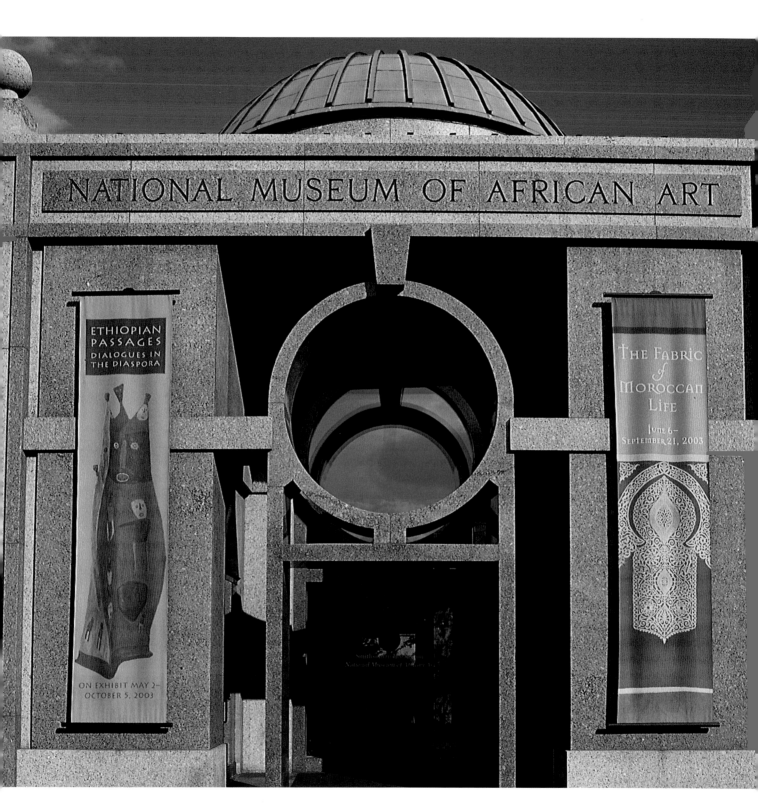

National Museum of African Art
Smithsonian Institution

This unique building is home to an impressive collection of the diverse and colorful artistic expressions found throughout Africa from ancient times through the works of contemporary artists. The collection ranges from paintings, printmaking, ceramics, furniture and tools to masks, figures, sculptures, textiles and musical instruments.

TOP

National Gallery of Art

The entrance to the East Building of the art gallery
announces the modern art treasures inside with this
colossal abstract bronze by Henry Moore titled *Knife
Edge Mirror Two Piece.*

BOTTOM

Sculpture at the Hirschorn Museum

The Sculpture Garden provides a contemplative haven
for viewing over 60 large-scale works of art from the
1880's to the 1960's.

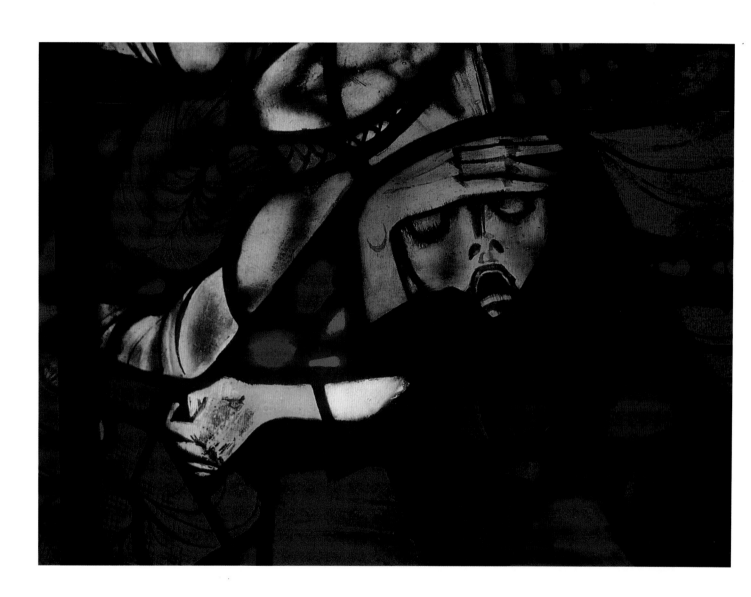

National Cathedral Stained Glass

The Cathedral Church of Saint Peter and Saint Paul boasts 215 spectacular stained glass windows. The largest is the 26-foot-diameter Rose Creation window (*page 82*). This majestic limestone cathedral was the longest-running construction site in the history of Washington. The final completion of the church's west towers in 1990 marked the end of 83 years of construction. And it has been well worth the wait.

Its mammoth size—the length of two football fields with towers that rise 30 stories tall— is fitting for its mission as a place for people of all faiths and nations to come and worship. (*Additional photos, pages 64 and 81*)

U.S. Capitol at Night

The majestic Capitol building dominates the nighttime sky. Congress soon passed a law ensuring that no other structure in Washington would stand taller than the Capitol. The construction of this important symbol of the new United States took 34 years to complete. As the nation grew, so did the need for a bigger building. The Capitol Extension dwarfed the original structure and dramatically changed its appearance as more exuberant Victorian design elements replaced Neoclassical sedateness.

THEY HAVE GIVEN THEIR
SONS TO THE MILITARY
SERVICES. THEY HAVE
STOKED THE FURNACES
AND HURRIED THE
FACTORY WHEELS. THEY
HAVE MADE THE PLANES
AND WELDED THE TANKS,
RIVETED THE SHIPS AND
ROLLED THE SHELLS.

PRESIDENT FRANKLIN D. ROOSEVELT

National World War II Memorial

Located on the National Mall, the National World
War II Memorial is the first national memorial
dedicated to all who served during World War II.

Freedom Plaza

Originally known as Western Plaza, Freedom Plaza was renamed in honor of Dr. Martin Luther King, Jr. A time capsule containing a few of his personal belongings is located at the southwest end of the plaza. Today it is often the site of political rallies.

ABOVE

Underground Metro Station

The Washington Metro is a 103-mile rapid transit system serving Washington and the surrounding areas of Maryland and Virginia. One of the largest public-works projects ever built, Metro is the second-busiest rail transit system in the United States.

OPPOSITE

Science Museum of the National Academy of Sciences

The museum's state-of-the-art, interactive exhibits engage visitors in current scientific issues that shape our lives. The museum was conceived by molecular biologist Daniel Koshland, in memory of his wife, Marian Koshland, an immunologist and molecular biologist.

ABOVE

Fresh Crabs
Marine Avenue Waterfront

Seafood lovers find the freshest catch, including these popular Maryland crabs, at open-air stands along the Maine Avenue waterfront.

Climbing on The Lincoln Memorial

McGuire was shooting photos near the reflecting pool
in the early morning twilight when he spotted a young
fellow climbing on Lincoln. There were no tourists or
park rangers around so he had the memorial to himself.
Lincoln's expression seems as if he is actually watching
his progress. McGuire later had the framed photo on
display at DC's Eastern Market when a woman
approached and said she tried climbing on Lincoln,
too, but got caught. He asked her what was the fine.
She said, $100. McGuire then asked her what was the
charge? She said the Park Police wrote on the ticket,
"Mounting a National Memorial."